HARVEST HOUSE PUBLISHERS
EUGENE, OREGON

Beneath His Wings

Eugene, Oregon 97402

ISBN 0-7369-0115-9

Art Uniq'
P.O. Box 3085
Cookeville, TN 38502
800-223-5020

Design and production by Garborg Design Works

Harvest House Publishers has made every effort to trace the ownership of all poems and quotes. In the event of a question arising from the use of a poem or quote, we regret any error made and will be pleased to make the necessary correction in future editions of this book.

Printed in China.

00 01 02 03 04 05 06 07 08 / PP / 10 9 8 7 6 5 4 3 2

Be not dismay'd whate'er betide,
God will take care of you;
Beneath His wings of love abide,
God will take care of you.

CIVILLA D. MARTIN

Under His wings I am safely abiding,

Tho the night deepens and tempests are wild;

Still I can trust Him, I know He will keep me,

He has redeemed me and I am His child.

Under His wings, under His wings,

Who from His love can sever?

Under His wings my soul shall abide,

Safely abide forever.

William O. Cushing

He will cover you with his feathers
and under his wings you will find refuge.

THE BOOK OF PSALMS

All day long the birds are singing
Sweetest songs that seem to rise
From their tiny throats far-reaching,
Even to the distant skies.

Then at night they rest securely,
Nestled close within their nest,
And the Father safely watches
Every little feathered breast.

Likewise we when night approaches,
Lay our weary heads to rest,
For we know that God will watch us
as He does the bird's wee nest.

JOSEPHINE CURRIER

All things living He doth feed;
His full hand supplies their need:
For His mercies shall endure,
Ever faithful, ever sure.

Let us then with gladsome mind
Praise the Lord, for He is kind:
For His mercies shall endure,
Ever faithful, ever sure.

John Milton

Carolyn Shores Wright
©97

Do not worry about your life, what you will eat or drink; or about your body, what you will wear... Look at the birds of the air; they do not sow or reap or store away in barns, and yet your heavenly Father feeds them. Are you not much more valuable than they?

THE BOOK OF MATTHEW

The Lord watches over you—the Lord is your shade at your right hand... The Lord will keep you from all harm—he will watch over your life.

THE BOOK OF PSALMS

God is our refuge and strength, an ever-present help in trouble.

THE BOOK OF PSALMS

I need Thee every hour;

Most gracious Lord;

No tender voice like Thine

Can peace afford.

I need Thee, O I need Thee,

Every hour I need Thee;

O bless me now, my Saviour,

I come to Thee.

Annie S. Hawkes

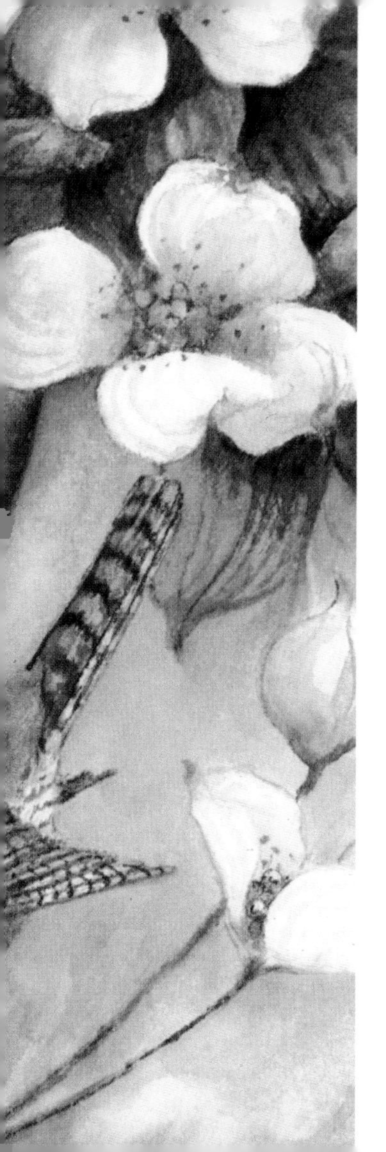

Tell. . .that though the earth's pillars shake, God is a refuge for us; tell the mourner that the everlasting God faileth not, neither is weary.

Charles Spurgeon

Blessed are those who mourn,
for they shall be comforted.

THE BOOK OF MATTHEW

O love that will not let me go,
I rest my weary soul in Thee;
I give Thee back the life I owe,
That in Thine ocean depths its flow
May richer, fuller be.

GEORGE MATHIASON

My soul finds

rest in God alone...
THE BOOK OF PSALMS

Wherever at home I happen to be,
My little girl often calls out to me
In lisping sweet tones but few understand:
"Oh wait, mama dear, and take hold my hand."
Then placing her soft wee hand in my own,
She ventures in ways she dare not alone.
But trusting in me is willing to go,
And where I may lead her, asks not to know.

How often the thought is precious to me,
My Father's dear hand is so ready to be
Clasped closely with mine, to lead me safe through
the future of life, unknown and so new.
Believing that He is near to me to aid,
No clouds can arise to make me afraid.
My trust in His love as perfect may be,
As my little girl now places in me.

Josephine Currier

Carolyn Shores Wright

Carolyn Shores Wright
©94

The Lord is near to

all who call on him...

THE BOOK OF PSALMS

Come near to God,

and he will come near to you.

THE BOOK OF JAMES

Just when I need Him, Jesus is near,

Just when I falter, just when I fear;

Ready to help me, ready to cheer,

Just when I need Him most.

William C. Poole

Whom have I in heaven but Thee?
And besides Thee, I desire nothing on earth.
My flesh and my heart may fail,
But God is the strength of my heart and my portion forever.

THE BOOK OF PSALMS

O Lord, don't hold back your tender mercies from me! My only hope is in your love and faithfulness.

THE BOOK OF PSALMS

When peace, like a river, attendeth my way,
When sorrows like sea billows roll;
Whatever my lot, Thou hast taught me to say,
It is well, it is well with my soul.

Horatio G. Spafford

Peace I leave with you;
my peace I give you....
Do not let your hearts
be troubled and do not
be afraid.

THE BOOK
OF JOHN

The Lord longs to be gracious to you;

he rises to show you compassion.

THE BOOK OF ISAIAH

Because of the Lord's great love we are not consumed, for his compassions never fail. They are new every morning; great is your faithfulness.

THE BOOK OF LAMENTATIONS

Simply trusting every day,
Trusting through a stormy way;
Even when my faith is small,
Trusting Jesus, that is all.

Singing if my way is clear,
Praying if the path be drear;
If in danger, for Him call;
Trusting Jesus, that is all.

Edgar Page Stites

Trust in Him at all times,
O people;
Pour out your heart
before Him;
God is a refuge for us.

THE BOOK OF PSALMS

Said the Robin to the Sparrow:
"I should really like to know
Why these anxious human beings
Rush about and worry so."

Said the Sparrow to the Robin,
"Friend, I think that it must be,
That they have no heavenly Father,
Such as cares for you and me."

Elizabeth Cheney

Praise to the Lord, who o'er all things
so wonderfully reigneth
Shelters thee under His wings, yea,
so gently sustaineth!

JOACHIM NEANDER

I am he who will sustain you. I have made you and I will carry you; I will sustain you and I will rescue you.

THE BOOK OF ISAIAH

If I take the wings of the morning,

and dwell in the uttermost parts of the sea;

Even there shall thy hand lead me,

and thy right hand shall hold me.

The Book of Psalms

Go out into the darkness and put
your hand into the Hand of God.
That shall be to you better than light
and safer than a known way.

MINNIE LOUISE HASKINS

There is no grave on earth's broad chart
But has some bird to cheer it;
So hope sings on in every breast
Although we may not hear it;
And if today the heavy wind
Of sorrow is oppressing,
Perchance tomorrow's sun may bring
The weary heart a blessing.

ANONYMOUS

He gives strength to the weary and
increases the power of the weak.

THE BOOK
OF ISAIAH

My soul clings
to Thee;
Thy right hand
upholds me.

THE BOOK
OF PSALMS

When I remember Thee on my bed,
I meditate on Thee in the night watches,
For Thou hast been my help,
And in the shadow of Thy wings I sing for joy.

THE BOOK OF PSALMS

You are my hiding place;
you will protect me from
trouble and surround me
with songs of deliverance.

THE BOOK
OF PSALMS

Carolyn Shores Wright

Faith came singing into my room,
And other guests took flight.
Grief, anxiety, fear and gloom,
Sped out into the night.

I wondered that such peace could be,
But Faith said gently, "Don't you see,
That they can never live with me?"

ELIZABETH CHENEY

Fear not, neither be discouraged.

THE BOOK OF DEUTERONOMY

When a storm is raging fiercely,

And the clouds obscure the sky,

Then we think of God, our Father,

On whose help we can rely.

He will safely guide our footsteps,

As through life we onward go,

And will give us strength and courage

To resist the winds that blow.

In the autumn time He sends us

His beautiful colors rare,

And when winter comes, He shields us

With tender, loving care.

So whether the days seem gloomy

Or brim-full of light and cheer,

We know He is with us always,

And therefore have naught to fear.

Josephine Currier

Don't think so much
about who is for or against you,
rather give all your care,
that God be with you in
everything you do.

THOMAS À KEMPIS

May you be richly rewarded by the Lord...
under whose wings you have come to take refuge.

THE BOOK OF RUTH

Weave in faith and God
will find the thread.

PROVERB

Keep me as the apple of your eye;
Hide me in the shadow of your wings.

THE BOOK OF PSALMS

*As one whom his mother comforts,
so I will comfort you...*

THE BOOK OF ISAIAH

Our mighty God is called alongside as we suffer. Here is genuine comfort, personal assistance, deep involvement and infinite understanding.

Chuck Swindoll

I can face that which I must endure while in my Father's arms.

Miriam Brown

Carolyn Shores Wright

The eternal God is your
refuge, and underneath
are the everlasting arms.

THE BOOK OF
DEUTERONOMY

Carolyn Shores
©96

ALFRED, LORD TENNYSON

Weeping may endure for the night,

But joy comes in the morning.

THE BOOK OF PSALMS

Like an eagle that stirs up its nest

That hovers over its young,

He spread His wings and caught them,

He carried them on His pinions.

THE BOOK OF DEUTERONOMY

Have mercy on me, O God, have mercy on me,

for in you my soul takes refuge.

I will take refuge in the shadow of thy wings...

THE BOOK OF PSALMS

I have held many things in my hands

and lost them all; but the things I have placed

in God's hands, those I always possess.

EARLINE STEELBURG

"Because he loves me," says the Lord,
"I will rescue him; I will protect him,
for he acknowledges my name."

THE BOOK OF PSALMS

To flee unto God is the only stay which can support us in our afflictions, the only armor which renders us invisible.

John Calvin

Let me dwell in Thy tent forever;

Let me take refuge in the shadow of Thy wings.

The Book of Psalms

I, even I am He who comforts you.

The Book of Isaiah

Under His wings, under His wings,
Who from His love can sever?
Under His wings my soul shall abide,
Safely abide forever.

WILLIAM O. CUSHING

Come discover a place of comfort and compassion,
a shelter that offers security and a refuge that brings reassurance.
Underneath the loving cover of God's protective wings,
you'll experience the joyous peace that comes when you
place your heart in the hands of the heavenly Father.